ART AND CRAFT SKILLS

PRINTING

Susan Niner Janes

SEA-TO-SEA

Mankato Collingwood London

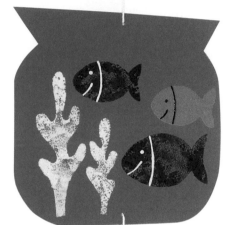

This edition first published in 2006 by
Sea-to-Sea Publications
1980 Lookout Drive
North Mankato
Minnesota 56003

Copyright © Sea-to-Sea Publications 2006

Printed in China

Library of Congress Cataloging-in-Publication Data

Janes, Susan Niner.
  Printing/ by Susan Niner Janes.
    p. cm.. − (Art and craft skills)
  Includes index.
  ISBN 1-932889-82-5
    1. Prints−Technique−Juvenile literature. I. Title. II. Art and craft skills
(North Mankato, Minn.)

NE860.J36 2005
760--dc22

2004063722

9 8 7 6 5 4 3 2

Published by arrangement with the Watts Publishing Group Ltd., London

Series editor: Kyla Barber
Designer: Lisa Nutt
Illustrator: Lynda Murray
Photographer: Steve Shott
Art director: Robert Walster

Contents

Getting Started

When you print you transfer color from one surface to another to create a pattern. Before you start, you need "the three Ps"... **p**rinters (objects to print with), **p**aper (or sometimes fabric or other materials), and **p**aint (or ink). You can decorate almost anything using the printing techniques described in this book.

Basic Printing Methods

1. **Relief printing** is using a raised surface to print, as in stamping or potato printing.

2. **Stenciling** is done by dabbing paint through a cutout shape in a piece of plastic or cardboard.

3. **Screen printing** is a way to stencil more complicated designs by sticking a stencil onto mesh, or net, that is stretched across a frame.

4. **Engraving** is carving or denting the printer to create a design. You can engrave a Styrofoam food tray. The carved parts show as white.

Think before you ink! Follow these tips for successful printing sessions:

★ Thick paint prints best—runny paint makes a mess.

★ Always take a test print—and correct any faults before the real print run.

★ To print an all-over pattern, measure out placement guidelines on your paper. Mark the lines (usually as boxes—a box grid) in pencil and erase them when the paint is dry.

★ Paper color affects paint color. It is usually best to print on a light-colored background. Test print first to check.

★ Always protect your work area with old newspapers. Sometimes this includes the floor as well as the tabletop.

★ Recycle it. Printing presents the perfect chance to recycle everyday items such as cardboard boxes and packing materials—to print on or with.

Trace and Transfer

Three steps to transfer a design:

1. Copy your design onto tracing paper.

2. Flip the design over and go over the outline in pencil.

Practice your transferring skills on this turtle—find out how to decorate it on page 23.

3. Turn the design back over to the right side and draw over the pencil outline once again, or rub down the design with the back of a spoon.

5

Printing Supplies

The basic items listed below include everything you will need to make prints. The store key shows you where to get them.

Store Key

Art supply store

Drug store

Supermarket

Craft store

Stationery store

Toy store

The Basics

1. Wax paper for low-cost tracing paper (🛒).

2. Metal ruler for measuring and cutting straight edges (🎨).

3. Scissors—use blunt-edged scissors for safety; small pointy ones for cutting stencils (✂️ 🎁 🎨).

4. Exacto craft knife—sometimes only a very sharp blade will do. Ask an adult to do the work (🎨).

5. Masking tape prevents your work from slipping as you print it (🎨).

6. White glue—the best all-around glue, with a strong bond (🎨🧸).

7. Glue stick for paper and cardboard (🎨✉️).

8. Black permanent-ink marker (fine point) won't run when it gets wet (🎨 🛒).

Paper, Cardboard, and Oaktag

9. White and colored paper, cardboard, and oaktag (or card stock if oaktag only comes in one color) (🎨🧸).

10. Scrap cardboard to cut on or use as printing board. Use boxes from (🛒).

11. Corrugated cardboard for printing texture or making stamps. Find it as packing material. Or buy it (🎨🧸).

6

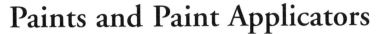

Paints and Paint Applicators

12. Acrylics are suitable for many surfaces including plastic and fabric. Read the label to determine washability of fabric ( ).

13. Poster paints are cheap and easy to find. Ready-mixed are best ( ).

14. Fabric paints are expensive, but you may have to use these if you want to machine wash the material once you have printed ( ).

15. Paintbrushes— use narrow ones for painting your designs, wide ones for backgrounds ( ).

16. Sponge rollers and brushes are useful for coloring large areas quickly ( ).

17. Sponges—for stenciling and making textures. Different types produce different effects ( ).

Tricks of the Trade

18. Clear plastic folders or looseleaf pockets make cheap stencil and printing material and paint palettes. Can be used as an alternative to acetate sheet, below. Cut the pocket into two separate sheets ( ).

19. Acetate sheet can be used for monoprinting and comb-transfer printing. Wash it after printing so you can use it more than once ( ).

20. Craft foam is useful for making stamps ( ).

21. Styrofoam food trays make good printing plates and disposable palettes ( ).

22. Thick felt-tip pens—use for inking stamps ( ).

23. Serrated scissors are good f or tidying edges ( ).

Keep It Tidy!

Make sure you have these things at hand before you start—

- ◎ An old T-shirt or adult-sized shirt—instant artist's smock.
- ◎ Old newspapers for protecting work surfaces.
- ◎ Clean rags, old towels, or paper towels.
- ◎ Liquid soap.

Stamping

Stamps are good for producing repeating patterns. They are easy to make from craft foam, cardboard, or kitchen sponge. Remember to keep the designs simple. Try the bird shapes below.

1. Sketch your designs on paper—keep them simple—you can draw details on the print later. Also, remember the design will print in reverse.

2. Transfer or copy the design onto the craft foam. Cut it out and glue it onto the oaktag. If you want to use two colors, mark out the dividing line with a pen.

3. Color in the raised part of the stamp with thick felt-tip pens. Tape your printing paper to a surface. Press the stamp firmly on the paper.

4. Lift the stamp off gently. You can complete the stamp print by drawing in the details (like the eyes and legs of the bird).

Note Card Holder

Cut out a birdhouse shape from cardboard. Cut an envelope in half and stamp designs on it. Then glue it to the oaktag and use it to store stamped note cards. Attach a cardboard loop to hold a pencil.

Now Try These

A Rainy Day
Stamps can be used to make simple clouds, umbrellas, and raindrops. Pick a theme and see how many stamps you can make to create a picture.

Flowers and Leaves
Use kitchen sponge to make simple flower shaped stamps. Use two different colors for the center and the petals.

Notepaper
To make personalized notepaper, stamp patterns along the edge of the paper.

9

Making Tracks

You have "instant printers" attached to your body—your hands and feet. Using them can be messy, so wear old clothes and keep a bucket of warm soapy water nearby. You can make your prints into boats, faces, animals, or even monsters by adding just a few details.

You will need:

- newspapers • bucket of water
- printing paper • glue stick
- acrylic or poster paints
- paintbrushes • liquid soap
- colored paper • scissors
- plastic tray (optional)
- old towels or rags • thread
- tape • wire hanger • tin can

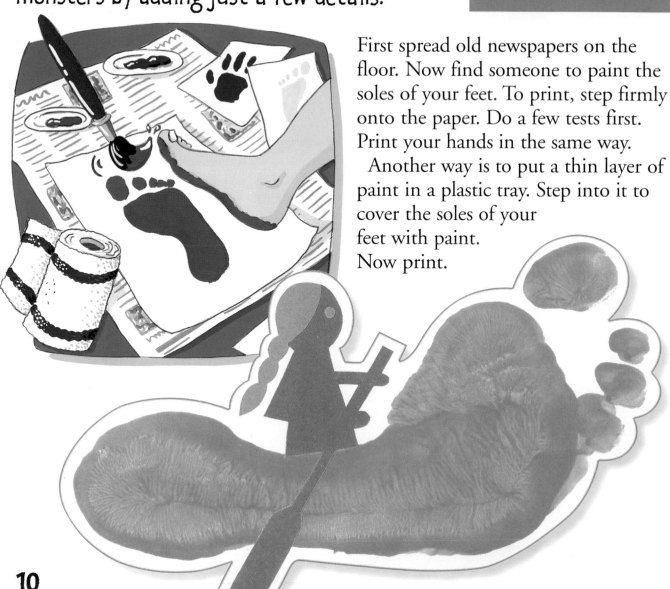

First spread old newspapers on the floor. Now find someone to paint the soles of your feet. To print, step firmly onto the paper. Do a few tests first. Print your hands in the same way.

Another way is to put a thin layer of paint in a plastic tray. Step into it to cover the soles of your feet with paint. Now print.

Adding Details

Making handprint and footprint pictures is like looking at clouds . . . there's no telling what your imagination will see. Glue on paper eyes, mouths, glasses, antennae, or clothes to make your prints come alive.

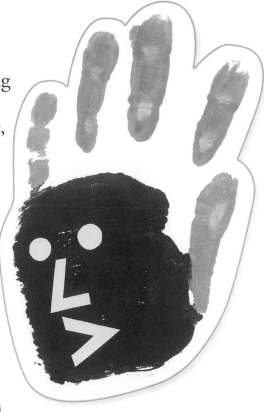

Now Try These

Alien Mobile

Make handprint and footprint pictures and decorate them by gluing on paper shapes. Make a small hole in the top of each print, and tie on thread. Attach the threads to a wire hanger to make a mobile.

Snail Tin

Make a footprint and paint on antennae. Cut it out and decorate by gluing on paper shapes. Paint a used tin can (cover any sharp edges with tape) and glue the snail on. Use it to store pens and pencils.

11

Anything Prints

If you can brush an object with paint, you can probably print with it. To make these puppets, print patterns using ordinary things found in the house.

The Basics

Remember to ask an adult's permission before printing with anything you find.

For many objects, all you have to do is brush on paint and stamp it onto the paper. Use thick and creamy paint.

To make small objects easier to handle, stick them onto oaktag with glue or poster putty.

To make an evenly spaced repeating pattern, you may want to measure out a pencil grid.

To print large surfaces, use bubble wrap or corrugated cardboard.

Always wash and dry the printers after use.

Jumbo Stick Puppets

Make lots of bold prints on paper. Now cut simple puppet shapes from oaktag. Cut out and glue your prints onto the shapes. Add faces. Tightly roll up a sheet of stiff paper to make a handle.

Printers Used Here:

Princess's coat: orange peel stuck onto cardboard.

Jester's mask: toy car tire and an eraser.

The big, bold patterns were printed with the ends of foam building bricks.

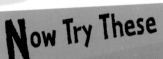

Jester's Mask
Print and cut out a mask and a hat, then glue them together. Glue paper "bells" onto the hat points.

Snail Spinner
Cut a snail shape from oaktag. Wind a piece of thick yarn or wool onto oaktag to make a stamp. Decorate the snail. Make a snail spinning top.

PRINTER'S TIP

◉ Poster paints may "bead up" on plastic. To make the paint stick, add a little liquid soap.

13

Sponge Stenciling

Cut a shape into oaktag or plastic, then sponge paint into the cut-out space. This is stenciling. The sponge creates a bubbly texture, just right for a fishy scene.

You will need:

* ★ clear plastic pockets
* ★ black permanent marker
* ★ acrylic or poster paints
* ★ colored oaktag
* ★ fabric paint
* ★ string
* ★ small scissors
* ★ sponges
* ★ paintbrush
* ★ masking tape
* ★ pencil
* ★ paper

1. Draw your design on a piece of paper. Cut a piece of plastic and slip the paper under it. Trace the design onto the plastic with a permanent marker.

2. Make a snip in the center of the plastic, then cut to reach the outline. Snip around the outline and remove the center. Make other sea-related stencils.

3. Tape the stencil in place. The see-through plastic makes it easy to position. Pour a little paint onto your palette. You may have to thin the paint with a drop or two of water. Use a paintbrush.

4. Cut some sponge and dip the end in the paint. Blot it on the palette, then dab paint into the stencil opening. Start at the edges of the stencil, taking care at corners, then do the center.

Fishy Mobile

Cut large sea-related shapes from colored oaktag. Using your stencils, decorate each shape and add details with fabric paint. Pierce holes in the oaktag shapes and join them with string.

PRINTER'S TIPS

★ Always remember to wipe your stencil before printing the next shape.
★ Try different sponges for different effects.

Now Try These

Fishy Cards
Draw a fish shape onto folded oaktag. Cut the fish out—take care not to cut the fold. Stencil on decoration.

Window Fishbowl
Cut a fishbowl hole in oaktag. Stencil fish onto a piece of clear plastic with acrylic paints. Tape it behind the fishbowl and hang it in the window.

Potato Prints

Potato printing is a quick and easy way to make clean, sharp prints. It is a kind of "relief" printing, which means printing with a raised surface. Carve different shapes and experiment with colors, patterns, or pictures.

You will need:

- craft knife ◆ acrylic paints or poster paints ◆ paintbrush ◆ paper
- drawing paper ◆ scissors ◆ black oaktag ◆ white glue ◆ large, clean potatoes ◆ kitchen knife ◆ straight pins ◆ pencils ◆ newspapers ◆ glitter
- paper towels ◆ plastic wrap ◆ cardboard ◆ fabric ◆ masking tape

1. Protect your work area with old newspapers. Cut the potato in half lengthwise. The cut surface must be flat and smooth.

ASK AN ADULT FOR HELP!

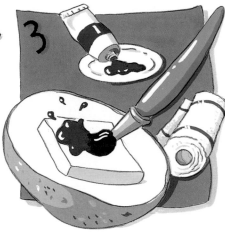

2. Design a pattern to fit on the potato surface and cut out a paper template. Fix in place with straight pins. Cut away the potato where you don't want it to print. Remove the template.

3. Blot the printing surface with paper towels to remove any juice (potato juice thins the paint and makes it slippery). Brush on the paint.

4. To print, press the potato block firmly, straight onto the paper. Then lift it off quickly and cleanly. You may be able to make a second print from one inking.

Magic Party Hat

Cut out a top hat shape from black-painted cardboard. Decorate a strip of paper with prints. Stick it on.

Glue a 2-foot strip (0.6 m) of oaktag onto the back of the hat, along the bottom edge. Glue the ends of the strip together to fit your head.

Now Try This

Pond Life

Print a complete picture using simple potato print shapes—fish, lily leaves, and flowers are easy things to start with. Try harder shapes when you feel confident.

Magician's Scarf

Take a scarf-sized piece of oaktag, cover it in plastic wrap, and tape a square of fabric tightly onto it. Print with glue instead of paint. Sprinkle glitter over the "glue prints."

Simple Engraving

Styrofoam trays used for packing supermarket food are ideal for making engraved printing blocks. To mark a picture in the soft material, simply press into it with a pointed tool. When the block is inked, the engraved outline shows as white or your paper color.

You will need:

- ★ Styrofoam food trays
- ★ a nail or sharp pencil
- ★ acrylic or poster paints
- ★ wide and thin paintbrushes
- ★ ballpoint pen
- ★ scissors
- ★ glue stick
- ★ paper
- ★ oaktag
- ★ stiff paper
- ★ masking tape
- ★ nail polish remover

1. If the tray has sides, cut them off. Plan your design on paper, then lightly pencil it onto the tray.

2. For a dotted outline use a nail or sharp pencil to punch holes along the outline. For a plain line, press firmly with a ballpoint pen.

3. Tape down the print block. Brush or sponge paint on evenly. Lay a piece of paper on top and smooth it gently. Lift the print off, then wipe the block clean.

Ship Cards

Print a ship on a piece of light-colored oaktag. Cut around the ship and glue it onto a piece of folded oaktag.

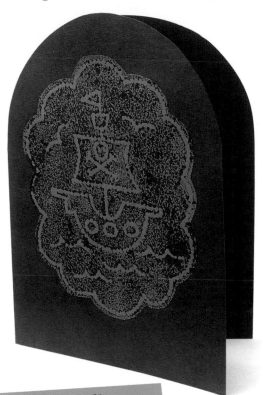

PRINTER'S TIPS

★ Try engraving your design into thick oaktag, or the back of oaktag for a similar effect.

★ Try printing with foam ceiling tiles—they come in a variety of textures. Ask an adult to help you cut them.

Now Try These

Bird
Make a bird print on stiff paper and cut it out. Cut a piece of paper and accordian fold it to make the wings. Use a pair of scissors and carefully make a slit in the center of the bird, and push the folded wings through.

Strawberry Notepad
Draw a strawberry onto Styrofoam with a thin brush dipped in nail polish remover. The Styrofoam will dissolve where you've brushed. The leaves at the top are stenciled.

ASK AN ADULT FOR HELP!

Only use nail polish remover when an adult is present.

Monoprints

Draw a simple line design on paper, slip it under a sheet of clear plastic, and you have created an instant printing press. Simply paint over the lines of your design and take a print. Try these simple lantern shapes first then experiment with more complex designs.

1. Draw a simple, two-colored design. This will be a printing guide—the monoprint will not be a perfect copy because the paint bleeds as it is printed.

2. Set up your "printing press": tape the design onto a piece of cardboard, then tape a piece of plastic on top.

3. Paint the lines of your design on the plastic, then lower a piece of paper on top. Smooth the paper lightly so the paint touches—don't press too hard.

4. Lift the print off carefully, then wipe the plastic clean. You are ready to start the next print.

Lantern Card

Print six lanterns on plain paper. Tear out each one. Thread them onto a piece of yarn, and glue them onto cardboard.

PRINTER'S TIPS

◎ Poster paints may "bead up" on plastic. To make the paint stick, add a little liquid soap.

◎ To make complicated, multicolored monoprints, print each color separately.

You must make sure that your paper is in the same position each time you print a new color. Draw lines on the plastic that match up with the corners of your printing paper.

Now Try These

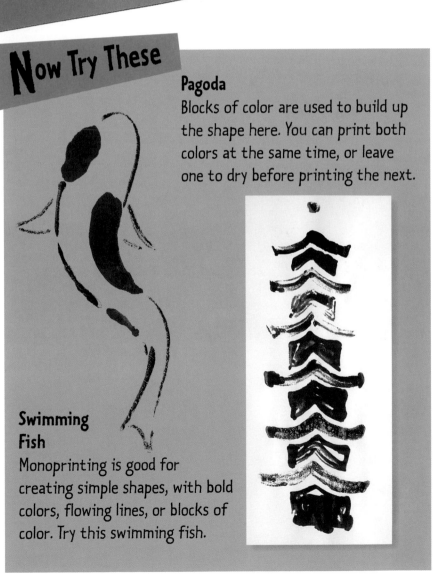

Pagoda

Blocks of color are used to build up the shape here. You can print both colors at the same time, or leave one to dry before printing the next.

Swimming Fish

Monoprinting is good for creating simple shapes, with bold colors, flowing lines, or blocks of color. Try this swimming fish.

Corrugated Quilling

These stamps, made from coiled strips of corrugated cardboard, create lacy patterns. The rolled shapes are inspired by the papercraft called "quilling." Each stamp can be used many times.

You will need:

- corrugated cardboard
- white glue • scissors
- glue stick
- colored oaktag and paper
- serrated scissors
- cardboard
- ruler
- pencil

Quilling Shape Chart

Cut a strip of corrugated cardboard, about 3 inches by 7 inches (8 cm by 18 cm). Curl the strip to make the shape you want.

Closed Shapes

Tight Coil: Roll the strip tightly. Glue the end.

Eye: Make a loose coil. Pinch opposite sides.

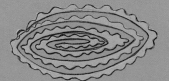

Teardrop: Make a loose coil. Pinch one side.

Square: Make a loose coil. Pinch to make four corners.

Loose Coil: Roll the strip loosely. Glue the end.

Triangle: Make a loose coil. Pinch to make three corners.

Open Shapes

Roller: Make a V-shape and roll each end outward.

Scroll: Take a strip, curl opposite ends toward center.

Heart: Pinch the scroll above to make a center V.

Ceremonial Elephant

Copy the elephant shape below onto colored oaktag, and cut it out. Cut out the ear and the tusk separately. Cut out a blanket in contrasting color oaktag. Use your corrugated stamps to print patterns. Glue on the blanket, tusk, and ear.

Now Try These

Mosaic Turtle
Copy or trace a turtle onto oaktag and cut it out. Cut tile shapes from a different-colored paper, and stamp them with a corrugated stamp. Glue them down to create the turtle's shell.

Jack's Vest
Print rows of pattern shapes on brightly colored papers. Cut out the rows. Cut out an oaktag person. Cut the rows to make up a vest shape, and glue them on the person.

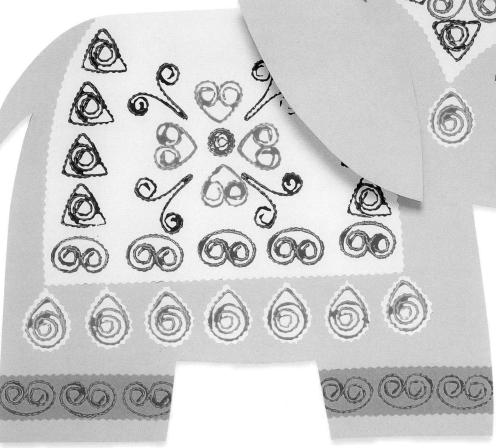

Roller Printing

Rollers are perfect for printing borders or for making allover patterns. Here are two types of rollers for you to make—pattern rollers and texture rollers.

You will need:

* ★ sponge rollers   ★ oaktag   ★ white glue
* ★ string   ★ ruler   ★ scissors
* ★ corrugated cardboard   ★ pencils
* ★ sheet of clear plastic   ★ cardboard
* ★ hole puncher   ★ felt
* ★ toilet paper tubes

Pattern Rollers

1. Take a toilet paper tube, trace the ends onto oaktag and cut two circles. Punch a hole in the center of each. Glue or tape the circles onto both ends of the tube. Push a pencil through.

2. Glue a strip of oaktag around the tube and trim it so the ends don't overlap. Draw three or four shapes on some oaktag and cut them out. Glue the oaktag shapes onto the roller. Space them evenly.

Texture Rollers

Corrugated Cardboard Roller
Make a basic roller (as before), then glue on corrugated cardboard.

Striped Sponge Roller
Tie a bought sponge roller with pieces of string. It will print uneven stripes.

Picture Frames

Cut four strips of oaktag. Print them in a bold color using a corrugated cardboard roller. Glue the strips together, as shown. Stick on backing board, leaving one side unglued so you can slip in a picture.

Now Try These

More Frames
Decorate large envelopes with a textured roller, then a patterned roller. Cut out a space from the center to make room for a picture.

Friendship Bracelets
Cut strips of felt, less than an inch (2 cm) wide and slightly too short to reach around your wrist. Roller print the strips with various patterned rollers. Sew on ribbon ties and beads.

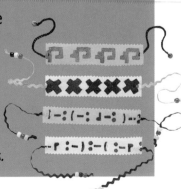

PRINTER'S TIP
★ Roller prints fade as you print. You can either leave the result as it is or touch it up with paint.

Combing

Using a cardboard comb, you can scrape paint off an inked surface to create swirls and zigzags. The print is then transferred to paper. Use this to print patterns, pictures, and even hairstyles.

You will need:

- a wide brush ◆ safety pins ◆ felt-tip pens
- colored paper ◆ scissors ◆ glue stick
- clear plastic sheet ◆ ribbon ◆ cardboard
- masking tape ◆ paper towels
- adhesive tape ◆ acrylic or poster paint

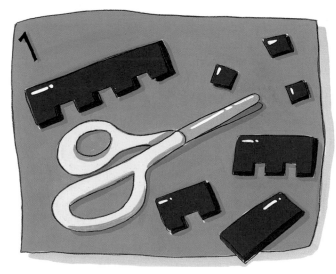

1. Cut out mini-combs from cardboard. Make combs with two, three, and four teeth. You will also need a few plain card scrapers without teeth.

2. Tape a plastic sheet onto a piece of cardboard. Brush on paint evenly. Now you are ready to comb your patterns.

3. Make squiggles, zigzags, or loops with the combs; straighter lines need simple strokes. For a bow, twist a plain piece of cardboard in the center.

4. To print, smooth a piece of paper over the pattern—don't press too hard. Peel the paper off quickly. Wipe the plastic, and you are ready to start again.

Badges

To make badges, snip out a hairstyle from the print and glue it onto cardboard. Add a paper cutout face. Cut around each badge. You can glue on a bow. Fix a safety pin to the back of the badge with a strip of adhesive tape.

Now Try This

Zebra
Use the combing method with black paint and white paper. Then cut out a zebra shape. You can add the mane and tail separately.

Printing Blocks

A printing block is a stamp that can be made up of different materials. Try to choose a variety of objects that will produce interesting textures when they are printed. For instance, the robot below is made from corrugated cardboard, craft foam, and oaktag.

You will need:

★ oaktag ★ white glue
★ corrugated cardboard
★ craft foam ★ brushes
★ masking tape ★ paper
★ acrylic or poster paints
★ pencil ★ scissors
★ star stickers ★ silver
marker ★ silver paint

1. Plan your design on paper—keep it bold and simple. Trace the design on to the oaktag.

2. Cut the shapes out of as many different materials as you can find, and glue them in place on the oaktag.

3. Tape the printing block down. Brush paint onto its raised parts. Work quickly so the paint doesn't dry.

4. Press paper onto the printing block and smooth it down. Don't miss any of the raised printing areas. Gently lift it off.

Robot in a Rocket

Print a robot and add details with silver marker. Cut a rocket-shaped hole from blue oaktag, add star stickers around the edge. Glue the robot print behind the hole.

Bits and Pieces

Glue wound string onto a block to make a balloon, add a basket from corrugated cardboard and clouds from bubble wrap. Take a print.

Pasta Bugs

Stick pasta shapes onto cardboard— perfect for insect prints.

Money Spider

Make a printing block out of coins. Wash your money when you've finished.

PRINTER'S TIP

★ Use printing materials that are textured and easy to cut: Styrofoam food trays, corrugated cardboard, and bubble wrap.

Screen Printing

Net stenciling is an easy type of screen printing and is good for printing fabric. You can also try printing a shape-within-a-stencil as with this T-shirt design.

You will need:

- cardboard
- stapler
- masking tape
- acrylic or fabric paints
- black paper
- self-adhesive plastic
- plain cotton T-shirt
- craft knife
- pencil
- ruler
- clothespins
- plastic wrap
- sponge
- paper
- net fabric
- paper clamps

ASK AN ADULT FOR HELP!

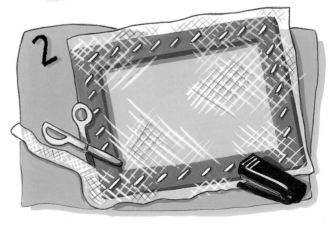

1. Plan your stencil design on paper. Ask an adult to cut out a window shape in thick cardboard, using a craft knife and ruler. The cardboard frame must be larger than your stencil design.

2. Cut a piece of net slightly larger around than the frame. Staple the net onto the frame. The net should be completely tight. Trim the net around the frame.

30

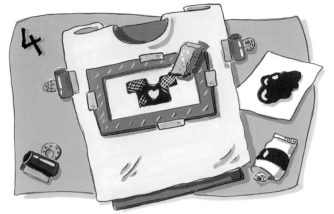

3. Trace the design onto self-adhesive plastic. Snip into the plastic and cut around line. Now snip out the center shape (here a heart) and keep it. Peel the backing off the plastic and smooth the stencil onto the net. Stick on the center shape too. The areas of mesh that are not covered with plastic will print.

"Triple-T" T-Shirt

You can make a net stencil for three different stencil designs. Print each in a different color in a row on your T-shirt. Wait until each print is dry before going on to the next.

PRINTER'S TIP

◆ If the net clogs up, clear it with a pin.

4. To print a T-shirt, first insert a piece of plastic-wrapped cardboard to keep it taut. Take up any slack material with clothespins. Tape on the stencil, then sponge on the paint. Remove the tape and carefully lift off the stencil.

Now Try These

Decorate Your Gym Bag

You can use net stenciling to print on your gym bag. Use the T-shirt stencil to decorate your bag. The shorts are made from ordinary plastic stencils (see page 14).

Fire! Make a fiery net stencil and dab yellow paint through the openings onto black paper. When dry, repeat using orange then red paint. Move your stencil each time you print.

Glossary

comb printing Cardboard combs can be used to make patterns and swirls in paint. The combed patterns create interesting prints (pages 26–27).

engraving Create a pattern by carving or pressing into a soft material, such as Styrofoam or thick cardboard. When you make a print, the pattern shows up as white, or the color of your paper (pages 4, 18–19).

monoprinting A print made from painting a flat surface, then transferring the paint to paper. As the pattern is repainted each time, every monoprint is slightly different (pages 20–21).

potato printing A raised shape can be created by carving into a halved potato. It can then be used as a printing stamp (pages 16–17).

printing Paint is transferred from one surface to another.

printing block A pattern is made by gluing lots of different materials onto oaktag. The raised surface is painted and used for printing (pages 28–29).

roller printing A roller can make interesting prints. You can add a textured surface to the roller, or shapes cut from oaktag, so that the roller makes a pattern as it goes (pages 24–25).

screen printing A stencil is made from either cardboard or plastic and stuck onto a mesh-covered frame. The mesh or net is then painted. You can use this technique to print on fabric (pages 30–31).

sponge stenciling A stencil is cut out of cardboard or plastic. Paint is sponged onto the paper through the stencil opening (pages 14–15).

stamping Simple shapes cut from cardboard or craft foam are stuck onto a piece of backing cardboard. The raised surface is covered with paint or ink, and used to print shapes (pages 8–9, 12, 22–23).

Index

Robin walks the rows to make sure everyone's in bed,

Pulls a worm up in his bill,

Cocks his head,

Now all is still.

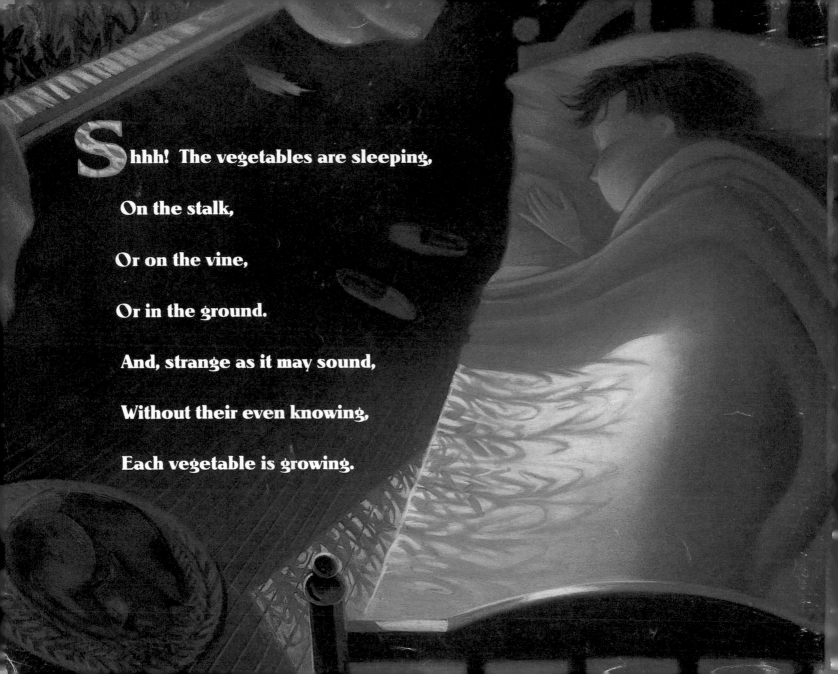

Shhh! The vegetables are sleeping,

On the stalk,

Or on the vine,

Or in the ground.

And, strange as it may sound,

Without their even knowing,

Each vegetable is growing.